HAM RADIO

The Complete Study Guide with Tips and Tricks for Beginners to Master Ham Radio Basics and Setup Like A Pro

Curtis
Campbell

Disclaimer

The information in this book is based on personal experience and anecdotal evidence. Although the author has made every attempt to achieve an accuracy of the information gathered in this book, they make no representation or warranties concerning the accuracy or completeness of the contents of this book. Your circumstances may not be suited to some illustrations in this book.

The author disclaims any liability arising directly or indirectly from the use of this book. Readers are encouraged to seek Medical. Accounting, legal, or professional help when required.

This guide is for informational purposes only, and the author does not accept any responsibilities for any liabilities resulting from the use of this information. While every attempt has been made to verify the information provided here, the author cannot assume any responsibility for errors, inaccuracies or omission.

Printed in the United States of America

Table of Contents

INTRODUCTION

If you are in search of the best way to communicate with friends and family, you should consider obtaining or building your own HAM radio station. Like mentioned during the course of this guide, HAM radio is a device that allows you to communicate and interact with friends and family members through phonetic alphabets and English from all around the world.

Before using a HAM radio, you need to ensure you get a HAM radio license because it allows you to operate the device legally and without any government interference. The essence of this guide cannot be overemphasized as there are a lot of things to learn.

Since several people are looking for a means to communicate with the people they like and want without hoping on their local service network, this device might just be the perfect alternative. HAM radio is filled with numerous and exciting features that will get you excited and running to the store to purchase the device and obtain a license.

CHAPTER ONE

Meaning of HAM Radio

HAM radio or Amateur radio can be defined as the
adoption of radio frequency spectrum wholly for
non-commercial purposes and is designed for the
exchange of messages, emergency
communication, self-training, private recreation,
radiosport, contesting, and wireless
experimentation. The emphases on non-
commercial/not-for-profit have partly given rise to

the specification of the term **"amateur"** which simply means that the operator who is interested in radioelectric practice must be authorized and duly licensed to engage in the non-commercial broadcasting, without commercial motives whether directly or indirectly. The wider implication of non-commercial broadcasting is that it must be differentiated from commercial broadcasting, public safety, like fire service and police, or other two-way radio services as used in the maritime, aviation, cab services, etc.

To bring it home, HAM radio, in a nutshell, can be described in the following four points:

1. It is a non-commercial, not-for-profit adventurous use of radios similar to walkie-talkies used by police, fire service officials, or the FBI.

2. HAM radio is a high-tech hobby, scientific and indeed fun which is enjoyed by fun-loving people all over the world.

3. Amateur Radio, also called HAM radio is a communication system, used for experimentation and thereby encourages learning.

4. HAMs deploy their skills and vast knowledge for the use of society particularly in times of natural disasters and wars.

How to install HAM Radio

Installing a HAM radio may pose some challenges because most installations are unique and different from others. But by observing the following 3 step installation, you are not likely to go wrong.

Step 1: Determine where to install it

In making this decision, there are certain things to consider before installing a HAM in a vehicle. This becomes necessary because the size of the transceivers and the mounting positions in the vehicle are usually restricted.

- The transceiver is capable of being useable

- It must be free from the operation of the vehicle

- It must be free from interfering with the airbag or other safety equipment.

- It must be located in a place with no direct access to the sun, heat output, etc.

- It must not constitute a hazard to the driver, including other occupants of the vehicle.

Step 2: Decide how to mount it

If you apply creativity, the process of mounting your transceiver is going to fall in place. So if you make up your mind to install it on your fold-down seatback, it is as simple as bending a piece of flat aluminum stock in sort of a V shape. The V shape when split, one part should go between the top of the seat and the headrest, and the other part kept some of the aluminum angles while holding the transceiver.

It makes too to ensure that the transceiver is mounted, enough room is available to allow plenty of airflows all over the heat sinks at the rear of the rig.

As it is very likely that when the transceiver is mounted to the bracket, you need to slide the bracket into place, and there the rig is held securely.

Step 3: It is done

The installation can be classified properly done if the transceiver is located without any interference and yet is exposed.

Equipment used for operating it

For you to operate as a HAM, you need the equipment that will enable you to achieve your goal. Over the years, HAM equipment has changed and new equipment has replaced old ones. One example is the use of voice over internet protocol (VoIP) which has become used today and has produced new types of ham radio equipment. So it behooves those nursing the ambition of becoming a HAM to decide on the type of frequency and communication method that will deliver the goods.

In the market, there are various types of HAM radio equipment available, and some of them offer great value, as well as being reliable. Buying new HAM equipment is generally preferred since it offers considerable advantages but thought at an extra cost.

Define your requirements

But first things first, it is important to determine the type of equipment that is needed from the outset before committing resources. There are various types of equipment used in HAM radio which may include the following:

- Transmitters
- Radio and Receivers (handheld, mobile, or mounted)

- HF transceivers

- VHF / UHF handhelds

- SWR meters

- Antennas

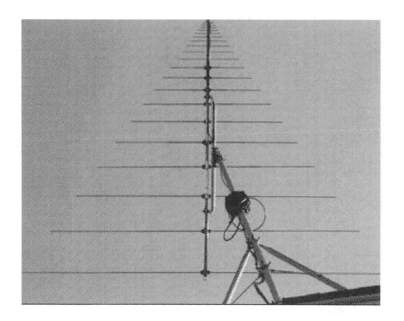

Depending upon what you may want to achieve, you may also decide to include computers, power cables, weather stations, towers, two-way radios, and some other specialized devices.

If you determine in advance what equipment you would need, it saves you some troubles. Some equipment such as transceivers you may decide whether to include bands to be covered, power output, modes of operation – FM, SSB, digimodes, etc., receiver filter makes and requirements, general facilities needed size and the likelihood of portable mobile operation.

Having a list of the possible equipment needed for the operations, it is imperative to look at reviews on the internet, magazines/journal, or friends who may know the particular equipment you might learn from. But before making up your mind, you must do a thorough investigation on each of the items.

Before you commit resources to the equipment, it is also vital to weigh the advantages and disadvantages of buying them new or fairly used. Brand new items will be more reliable than second hand, but will definitely cost more. Preferably, you should go for brand new equipment since its durability can be guaranteed. Used HAM radio equipment can also offer a reasonable solution, but there are drawbacks if you decide to tow that route. They include the following:

- Used HAM radio equipment is typically outside the manufacturer's warranty period.

- The used equipment may be defective that is hidden.

- The service agreement of the used equipment may have expired.

- The used equipment may have significantly been overtaken by the new equipment while the expiry date of the used equipment may be close. In this case, the used equipment may no longer be efficient.

- If the used equipment has been refurbished, and the refurbishment is not properly done, the problem if not discovered at the time of purchase, may linger on until it is phased out.

CHAPTER TWO

How to connect the Antenna

Different guidelines apply to different Antenna installations. Ham radio antenna can be used, others such as domestic television antenna or CB could also be used.

It doesn't really matter the type of antenna, what is important is the connection to ensure the best performance is achieved. But before the connection takes place, there are a variety of things to be considered such as:

- **Location for the antenna:** For the antenna to operate optimally, it should be visible all around it. To achieve this, other nearby objects should not interfere or block it so that the maximum amount of signal should reach or leave the antenna.

- **Points to anchor the antenna:** Anchor points on the house such as chimneys or even trees can serve as a suitable anchor place for the antenna. Horizontal antennas usually need anchor points at either end.

- **Inside or outside antenna:** Find out which one works better for you – internal or external antenna. An external antenna as a matter of fact works better because it can further from objects that can introduce loss or detune the antenna.

- **Antenna height:** The antenna height should be considered to ensure that an appropriate height is selected to enable optimal performance.

- **Interference consideration:** HAM radio station antenna should be kept away from possible interference, and as a result, it should be kept in mind.

- **HAM radio transmitter:** This should be kept away from domestic appliances since proximity can cause possible interference.

- **Antenna matching:** For the HAM radio antenna to operate effectively, it must match the feeder. Indeed all radio frequency systems (antenna, feeder, transmitter, and receiver) must be consonant since they all have some characteristic impedance.

How to operate the Antenna

One of the challenges in operating a HAM radio is the choice of antenna that serves the best purpose under given conditions. Users are divided making these choices – some HAMs prefer the large directive antenna on a high tower, but other antenna users due to some limitations imposed by space make other choices a compromise. Consequently, because of these limitations, a compromise antenna has to be selected, leading to further experimentations.

EFHW antenna

This antenna is the choice of many HAMs because of its harmonic relationship of the higher frequency bands since it performs as multiple numbers of half wavelengths on these bands. The RF transformer, known as an anun can match from an unbalanced line to an unbalanced antenna. Since it is a high impedance antenna, it doesn't require an earth connection.

This type of antenna offers low-cost advantages as well as multiband operations but has the limitation of a higher level of interference than balanced antennas and requires ATU in addition.

Wire dipole

The dipole is a cost-effective antenna and is widely used for radio communications. Its performance can be very good if it is mounted further high in a suitable place. Because the length of the dipole regulates the frequency of operation, this limits its use as it can be used with only one band. But it is possible to have other versions that can be used for HF multiple-band operations.

About call signs

A call sign is a distinctive code, given to HAMs by the licensing issuing authority which identifies each HAM operator in every station location. It also serves to recognize HAMs when dealing and communicating with other HAMs

The first part of the call sign (prefix) represents the country the operator is broadcasting while the last part (suffix) represents the individual operator. The suffix consists of about three alphabets and in the absence of it, monitoring of individual stations across the globe cannot be monitored.

Buyers guide on HAM Radio

The good thing about HAM radio is that when other means of communication fail especially in times of emergency, it is still possible for people to keep on talking. It is also affordable and not very difficult to operate

Despite the fact there is a whole range of HAM radios available in the marketplace; the difficulty in making the right selection can't be over-emphasized. The following are some of the best the market can provide.

1. BTECH DMR-6X2 Dual Ham Radio

If you want a dual-band radio that is capable of holding up to 200,000 contacts, 10,000 talk groups including 4,000 stores, you can opt for BTECH DMR-66X2 because it is capable of doing that and even more. Ad-hoc-call which may not be saved in memory or radio channel can also be enabled

2. BaoFeng UV-82 High Power Dual Band Ham Radio

This is also a dual-band radio that enables you to communicate in two separate frequencies but could be very powerful; though made in China, but the good thing is that while under warranty if anything goes wrong, it will get replaced if you are in the US.

3. Greaval UV-5R 8W 2-Way Dual Band Ham Radio

If you are looking for a cheaper HAM radio that competes with the more expensive ones in terms of features and accessories, BaoFeng UV-82 is the choice. These are in addition to long battery duration.

4. Radioddity GD-77 DMR Amateur Ham Radio

The Radioddity GD-77 DMR is a two-way radio communication system and solidly built. The built-in features together with the high-capacity battery put it ahead of its peers in its price range.

5. TYT TH-9800 PLUS Version Quad Amateur Base Station

With the 4 Band radio, and having received the FCC approval, it is the toast of many HAMs. More importantly, it is at the price range any HAMs can afford and you will have no reason to use a 2 band when the 4 band is affordable.

6. Xiegu G90 HF Amateur Radio Transceiver

If you are the type that goes for flashy wares, Xiegu G90 HF Ham radio should be your choice. Its features include a detachable head unit that can be anchored anywhere of your choice. But it is pricey but some HAMs say it is value for money.

7. Icom IC-7 HF All Band Amateur Base Transceiver

If you are a newbie and need a ham radio that is relatively simple to operate, then go for Icom IC-7 HF. Moreover, it has the capacity of accessing HF, which is why it is relatively high in price. It rugged and capable of withstanding the test of time.

The challenge posed by buying the right Ham radio is the availability of so many brands in the market. But if you can define what you are buying and the features that come with them, you will be in a better position to make the right choice. Also, when purchasing ham radio, some pieces of equipment come with them, so be smart to know these four pieces of equipment that should be included in your package. They include:

- Transceiver – the combination of receiver and transmitter
- Power supply – to power the transceiver
- Antenna – for good reception.
- Antenna tuner – to match the antenna and the transceiver for better reception all the time.

CHAPTER THREE

How to use a Transceiver

Transceivers are special kinds of radio-based communication systems. They help to hasten rescue efforts in a local area. Users can learn how to use a transceiver by understanding the process of setting up a HAM radio.

Besides, you will find out that most radio sets that are sold can only receive and transmit radio frequencies in one bearing. The ideal mode to increase the range of an individual radio set utilizes a dual-band radio receiver or transmitter. All the same, a dual-band set will not receive or transmit in both UHF and VHF bands.

If you choose to make a HAM radio station, it is often recommended to work on the features of the operating environment, because the weather is something that can be changed. While making your HAM radio station and the frequency, you won't escape using some major functions like modulation and fixed radio frequency. Furthermore, numerous kinds of frequency have been used for long periods, so it is always best to utilize a well-known frequency and it can be identified by a majority of HAM operators.

About Logbook

In order to maintain records of account of what goes on the radio by HAMs, Logbooks are kept for this purpose. These accounts maintain a dual purpose - an official as well as a personal purpose.

To verify your communication by the authorities, the logbook gives the authorities a full account of how you operate.

The logbook can also represent your personal radio history which accounts for the people and places you have had a conversation with and the role you played.

About HAM Radio power supply

The Ham radio systems use 13.8-volt power. But different system's amperage changes significantly between systems which mean the higher the amperage the higher your signal will be. If you choose to go for a small handheld receiver, it is recommended that you make use of the built-in battery unless you don't want to use it but opt for an alternative power supply. In that case, you can purchase an inexpensive 3 amps power supply that will serve your purpose.

If your transceiver is large, you will definitely need more power. But one thing you should look out for is that some transceivers are procured with a power supply while others don't. Whatever the case maybe, find out from the specifications so that you know exactly what you are bargaining for. Normally, if your system is a little bit powerful, the minimum power requirement is 20 amps if you want to reach maximum performance.

Audio

HAM radio digital audio modes can take different shapes and usually they are used on VHF/UHF, but when used on HF tremendous advantages can be gained.

The challenge posed by the digital voice systems is that there are many from which to choose from and as a result, there is no one standard for all.

Most receivers can easily work FM, AM, and SSB but for Ham radio, there is no standard. Moreover, Ham radio equipment for digital voice is hardly multi-standard.

Though it has been observed that digital voice appears to be commonly used on VHF/UHF than HF but other digital voice systems can be used on HF.

When it comes to Ham radio digital voice, the solution is to use a PC that links into the HF transceiver. With this method, Sound out of the sound card or audio output drives the audio input and it is ultimately transmitted.

CHAPTER FOUR

Using QSL Cards

Typically, it is normal for HAMs to despatch QSL cards as an indication and documentary evidence of the initial contact. The cards are vital and are self-designed. They usually contain information that includes the following:

1. Name and address of HAMs operator.

2. Name of the station which sends the QSL card.

3. Date and time the contact is made.

4. Frequency of contact

5. Report of the signal exchange.

6. Input power

7. Equipment type and type of antenna.

8. Other comments.

Typically, QSL Cards are sent directly but also can be sent through the QSL Bureau. HAMs run QSL bureaus in all the countries which collect and send QSL cards in a very economical way. A QSL card is easy to design and you can design your card.

About Morse Code

Morse code relates to a technique used in telecommunication whereby text characters are coded on a standardized format of two different signal durations known as dots and dashes.

International Morse Code encodes the 26 English alphabets without distinguishing between lower and upper case letters. The Morse code symbol is formed sequentially using dots and dashes. The dot duration represents the central unit of time measurement in Morse code transmission. The duration of a dot 1/3 the duration of a dash and each dash or dot in a character is followed by a period of absence, known as space, equivalent to the dot of duration. The space of duration equal to three words separate the letters of a word, and the words are separated by a space equal to seven dots.

Morse code was created to improve the efficiency of encoding so that the span of each symbol is roughly opposite to the frequency of occurrence of the character that it stands for in the text of the English language. This means basically the most common English letter, the letter "E" code is the shortest, i.e a single dot.

Fundamentally, since Morse code essentials are measured by proportion rather than a specific time, the code is usually transmitted at the highest rate that the receiver can decode. The Morse code transmission speed is usually specified in words per minute

Morse code transmission is usually affected by on/off keying of an information-carrying medium, in this case – electric current, visible light, radio waves, or sound waves.

It is possible to commit to memory and Morse code indicates in a form the human senses can perceive such as sound waves or visible light, which can be interpreted by experts in this field.

In occasion of crises, Morse code can be created by improvised techniques, in this case, switching a light on and off, striking an object, or sounding a horn or whistle, which makes it one of the simplest and most versatile methods of telecommunication.

Learning with Morse code

People communicate via Morse code before telephones. The technology has been in existence for more than 160 years and still relevant today, particularly among HAMs. It is fun to learn Morse code and it is a hobby you can have and it can be engaging too.

It is like learning any language and to grab it fully, you practice it over and over again. The codes can be learned in different ways and some of those methods include the use of:

- Farnsworth method
- Kock method
- Mnemonics

Farnsworth method

Farnsworth method – this sends and receives letters and other symbols at their usual relative timing of the dots, dashes, and spaces. The initially overstated spaces between symbols are used to provide thinking time for the sound **"shape"** of the letters and symbols easier to learn. The spaces can be resized as you learn codes over time.

Koch method

The Koch method adopts the full target speed from the beginning but starts with two characters. As far as the strings holding the characters can be captured with 90% precision, more characters are added and with time, the full characters can be learned.

Mnemonics Method

This is the use of visual charts to learn Morse codes and it has been developed and used over many years back. It adopts the method that uses words or phrases that has a similar rhythm as a Morse character.

Tips: learning Morse codes

- Get familiar with the codes – One of the first things you have to do is to get familiar with the codes as to how they look like. If you prefer, print it out, commit it to memory as you learn it during your free time.

- Start listening to Morse codes – To begin to learn Morse code, you should start listening to it. Go online and download the app. Make sense of the letters you listen to.

- Use a nifty chart – Look for and find a nifty chart and copy it if possible, and then print it out. Follow the instructions – start off where it says **"start"**. Each time you hear a short sound, you move down and to the left. On the other hand, if you hear a long sound, you move down to the right.

- Practice with the AA9PW app. – This is an online application that helps you if you practice with it for about 10 minutes every day. You will be heading to becoming a Morse code expert. If you like, you can get at "The Mill", an app you can download. You can learn to use international Morse codes as well as the American Morse codes.

How to write with Morse code

Morse code is one way of transmitting text, via a series of distinctive sounds or light, represented by dots, dashes, or lines.

Morse code uses basic characters that make it simple to use in long-distance communication, Amateur, emergency, or improvised calls. Though it has proved difficult to learn since people prefer to use normal characters.

If you can read and write Morse code, it will probably improve your learning process. The codes can be constructed by applying the following transformations:

1. Replace dots with vertical lines
2. Maintain dashes as horizontal lines
3. Elements of a character are kept vertically in an up-to-down direction. Vertical lines are written from left to right. However, some characters have a second, more compact form which makes them arranged in both lefts

to right, and up to down. This applies to letters
C, F, and L.

CHAPTER FIVE

Understanding the Digital Mode

Amateur radio digital mode is becoming increasingly an important mode of transmission today. Digital mode has developed into different forms ranging from packet radio and RITY to WSJT, FT8, and others. The area that has grown significantly in Amateur radio since the introduction of PCs is the use of digital means of transmission. However, the digital mode has presented a fascinating way to transmit over ham radio, with associated challenges different from the more traditional modes of transmission.

How to use the digital modes

RTTY was initially thought of as the first of the digital modes but used as it were large and heavy mechanical teleprinters or teletypes. The introduction of computers in the home, however, made the teleprinters redundant, making space available, a commodity largely needed in ham radio stations.

The development in computer hardware and software together with the transmission technology has made it possible to employ some of the innovative techniques, and consequently, different digital modes of transmission modes have been developed. A vast number of different digital modes have sprung up, making it possible to match the right mode with the right application.

Variety of ways to use digital modes

Given below are some of the commonly used digital modes.

1. **RTTY – Radio Teletype:** Radiotele type was used earlier in the digital modes but it was fraught with large mechanical teleprinters or teletypes.

   In RTTY data was sent at the rate of either 45.5 or 50 bands while employing a two-tone scheme. Normally on HF, the carrier signal was frequency shift keyed, while on VHF and over an FM signal, it had an audio tone that was frequency shift keyed. Data would be sent on the strength of Baudot code rather than ASCII which applies to many transmissions today.

2. **Packet Radio:** In the case of packet radio, data are sent in packets, and once received by the other station, it is checked for completeness and accuracy of receipt. If

correctly received, another packet can be sent, otherwise if not, it has to be resent.

When the packet radio system is in operation, it lets the other number of facilities like digipeaters to send messages and the use of mailboxes, etc. Because of the length these packets present, this form of digital mode suits VHF/UHF rather than HF.

3. **AMTOR:** This digital mode represents one of the first computer-style modes to be used on HF. Data is normally sent out in small numbers, and once it is well received, the next number of data is despatched. By the way, the letters AMTOR stand for AMateur Telex Over Radio

This mode is suited to HF operation, where its use is highly recognized. However, since more sophisticated forms of digital mode such as PSK31 have been adopted in the airwave, AMTOR is being gradually pushed by the wayside.

4. **PSK31:** PSK31 name is coined from the modulation format and rate used. The modulation transmits data at a rate of 31 25 bits per second and it uses phase-shift keying (PSK).

   This amateur radio digital mode is popular with HF and it is tough to interference. It has gained acceptance because it allows real-time "chat" type contacts to happen as well as other advantages.

5. **PACTOR:** PACTOR is one of the digital mode schemes that combines elements of AMTOR and packet radio that uses frequency Shift Keying (FSK) modulation and is fundamentally used on the HF portion of the radio band.

   PACTOR was developed to enhance the reception of digital data during the period of the weak or noisy signal. It has the advantage of combining the bandwidth efficiency of packet radio with the error-correction and automatic repeat request of AMTOR

6. **CLOVER:** This is a digital communication mode that has the advantage of working with a narrow band HF communications. It enjoys the feature of monitoring the link between the transmitter and receiver and regulates the modulation format in accordance with requirements. CLOVER combines the sending of 8-bit digital data and carries ASCII text as data that can be executed without using the additional control characters normally required in other digital modes.

How to use the Digital Voice

Different voice modes are available today that are used within the amateur radio

Voice communication has become a popular format for amateur radio communication because it is simple and makes life comfortable to talk to people on a direct person-to-person basis through amateur radio.

The name radiotelephony in technical terms is given to voice communications over the radio, but sometimes it may be referred to simply as **"phone"**.

Several options these days are available that can be used to make voice or phone contact through amateur radio.

These available options are listed below:

1. Amplitude modulation, AM:

Amplitude modulation utilizes the amplitude of the signal to transmit the voice waveform, and it is also regarded as the original voice communication that came before radio, although it is no longer useful currently.

That doesn't mean Amplitude modulation is about to be abandoned, but more efficient modes that require less power at the same rate of performance are available. Having said that, you still find some HAMs using amplitude modulation, and most HF transceivers can transmit AM

2. Frequency modulation, FM:

The advantage of Frequency Modulation over several forms of communication applications including amateur radio is that instead of modulating the amplitude in the way of voice, the frequency is changed. Frequency modulation is very useful for mobile communication since the signal strength variations caused as a result of location changes can be reduced because the frequency variations are of the essence. For channelized communications on the VHF and UHF bands, FM is popular for many people.

3. Single Sideband, SSB:

Single Sideband derives from amplitude modulation and what happens is that the carrier and one sideband are reduced and this as a result enhances the spectral and power efficiency levels. Single sideband is primarily the voice mode that is used on the HF bands and to a lesser extent on the VHF and UHF. Bands.

4. Digital Voice Modes:

The digital voice modes, having been improved technologically over the last two decades ago or more, have several advantages over the analog modes in terms of performance. The spectral and power efficiency levels have been proved better and they can be copied at a very low signal level than what obtains in analogue. Though it is possible to use digital voice on any frequency, primarily it has been created for VHF and UHF bands where it carries similar traffic to that of FM. It is observed its primary main mode use is D-STAR and System Fusion or Fusion.

On the whole, it boils down to personal preference, but the license requirements in all cases must be complied with. But the licensing authorities do relax on the common digital voice modes, so it leaves you with an abundance of choice of amateur radio voice modes that can be used.

CHAPTER SIX

Q-Codes Terminologies

One way of explaining what Q-Code is all about is the use of abbreviation. A long word or sentence can be shortened so that it can be written quickly instead of a long sentence. For instance, you can recall the abbreviations used in SMS messages. It is typically the same. ASAP means As Soon As Possible.

In the same vein, Q-codes are similar for HAMs. HAMs have provided Q-codes to lessen the effort put in trying to communicate and make their conversations easier and faster.

Some of the Q-Codes used in communication are as follows:

QRA What is the name of your station?

QRL Are you busy?

QRV Are you ready?

QRZ Who is calling me?

QRT Shall I stop sending?

QTC How many telegrams do you have for me?

QTH What is your position in latitude and longitude?

QRI How is the tone of my transmission?

Understanding Radio phonetic alphabet

Phonetics

Phonetics are words that consist of the opposite of letters which are used instead of letters.

For example: If you want to say DAN using phonetics you should instead say: Delta, Alpha, and November.

Phonetics is particularly essential because the English alphabets are similar.

Voice-operated stations use the standard list of words to signify each letter since it is easier to use them to give the call Signs, name, location, etc. in adopting this approach; confusion would be avoided when exchanging messages.

Listed below are the standard phonetics as suggested by the International Telecommunication Union:

A: Alpha

B: Bravo

C: Charlie   M: Mike

D: Delta   N: November

E: Echo   O: Oscar

F: Foxtrot   P: Papa

G: Golf   Q: Quebec

H: Hotel   R: Romeo

I: India   S: Sierra

J: Juliet   T: Tango

K: Kilo   U: Uniform

I: India   V: Victor

K: Kilo   W: Whiskey

L: Lima   X: X-Ray

Y: Yankee   Z: Zulu

CHAPTER SEVEN

How to use Radio Phonetic Alphabet

The use of the radio phonetic alphabet cannot be overemphasized and it is needed because users are expected to utilize the phonetic alphabet when on air. When you are communicating on the air, using the Nato Phonetic alphabet can assist in preventing confusion that occurs due to many letters that sound the same.

The major idea here is to become familiar with standard phonetics and make use of them when operating sound. While using the radio phonetic alphabet, the HAM radio operators must also be error-free and conscious to avoid disruption and words must be pronounced accurately.

Where can it be used?

There are tons of places where the HAM radio phonetic alphabet can be used and they include the following:

- Police
- Armed forces
- Professional or expert communicators
- Emergency service
- Military

Making your first interaction with the CQ

At this point, you can now proceed to make your first interaction with the CQ. Once you turn the band, there are things you might probably hear like "CQ CQ CQ... This is Also Alpha Charlie Six Victor standing by the communication will be repeated three times. Therefore, this is the well-known method of initiating or starting a call.

Going further, the communication CQ is HAM radio short way for allowing individuals know that you are calling. The operator's call sign is the **"Alpha Charlie Six Victor"**. The call sign is the grouping of numbers and letters and it recognizes your station. Words are spoken so hard to understand letters will not be misunderstood, an example includes when the operator is making use of a call sign of AC6V. When spoken, you can use a generally accepted word for "A"," C", and "V" which means Alpha, Charlie, and Victor.

CHAPTER EIGHT

Instructions to follow before calling

CQ4

Perhaps if you want to call CQ3, you should endeavor to follow some steps which will ensure you are on the right path and so you won't make any mistake during the process. Meanwhile, before we get started, it is important to note that if you decide to call CQ4, you should be ready for anyone to answer the call.

Here are the instructions to follow before calling CQ4:

1. **Search for a clear frequency by sending "Is this frequency in use"**: In case it is on CW, ensure you use QRL. Then be patient for 30

seconds or more and send a similar message once more. Once the frequency becomes clear, move to the next step.

2. **Begin your call:** While starting your call, make sure you try it on three occasions.

3. After trying it on three occasions, be patient for about 30 seconds to 1 minute *(NB: In case no one replies to the call, you should then start once more from the beginning)*.

4. In a situation whereby the station returns to you but you are unsure of the call sign, make sure you avoid using the CW pro sign of QRZ. When this happens, use basic and simple English.

How to obtain your License

If you are ready to commence your HAM radio career, then you should consider obtaining your HAM radio license. Getting licensed will give you every right and control over owning your own HAM radio station and running it legally.

Meanwhile, if you seek to get your license, you will be issued with a test that will include knowledge in amateur radio regulations, rules, and electronic theory. Also, the three kinds of accessible or obtainable HAM radio licenses include:

1. **General:** With this license, you can get the entire advantages of the technician license added to the skill to be able to communicate on frequencies in the high-frequency band.

2. **Technician:** This is the ideal license for beginners. It includes 35 questions that will include questions related to basic electronics theory, and radio safety rules and regulations.

When you complete the available questions, you will be issued a license for communicating in UHF, VHF, as well as microwave frequency bands.

3. **Extra:** The extra license includes more than 700 questions and requires intense studying and learning. Meanwhile, if you get a pass mark, you will be allowed to use a general and technician license alongside access to exclusive sub-bands.

What is a short wave?

Shortwave is identified as a general term that describes any radio that uses roughly 1 MHz-30 MHz range, which includes shortwave listening, CB, and Ham Radio. More so, short wave listening consists of a broadcast shortwave. Ham radio can make use of shortwaves and speak to the world.

Going further, the short wave also consists of all the HAM frequencies (lower than VHF and UHF) and most of the frequencies in between.

CHAPTER NINE

Predicting a short wave propagation

Short wave propagation prediction models are usually learned, with major emphasis on the procedure of these models by the shortwave broadcast community. Their capability for forecasts is established to be restricted in the use of the monthly median.

Various developing technologies converse for the improvement of prediction models. Improvement from the prediction of short wave propagation may result from observations of coronal holes and other relevant solar features for long-term and short-term ionospheric predictions. The application of this class of measurements for adaptive HF broadcasting systems is also discussed *(NB: Finally, the integration of ray-tracing into propagation calculations in the prediction model is reflected upon).*

How to know a functional gray line operation

To know a functional gray line operation, users need to make use of VHF band 2 or UHF band 4. In addition, VHF frequency is normally found in the 5 to the 15-kilohertz range and the HF frequency can possibly be 70 to 300 megahertz range.

The radio movement in your home should be reduced in relation to the AMSAT-DL. In case the power is not turned on, you might not be allowed to transmit but you might be allowed to receive *(NB: This means you should only transmit when it is needed).*

Grayline operators can still maintain or operate but they will be speaking to one another like through a relay and not to the public. HAM radio reception on HAM frequencies might still be important, but do not forget that the gray line operators will also be needed.

Prior to knowing a functional gray line operation, you should as well know the rules and regulations about the gray line operator. These rules are so easy to identify, first of all, gray line operators are able to transmit and receive any other frequency from a PSTN. When the gray line operator is shifting aside from his allocated frequency, they would transfer to a different frequency after about 10 minutes.

CHAPTER TEN

Using Tropospheric Scatter

Tropospheric scatter is a way of interacting with microwave radio signals over a given distance.

Furthermore, the propagation method utilizes the tropospheric scatter, especially when radio waves are at SHF and UHF frequencies are casually distributed. A Tropospheric scatter system can actually reach large distances.

The use of tropospheric scatter is very important in HAM radios because of the distance its covers during communication and it can also be useful during a weather change period *(NB: This is because the weather favors communication signal)*.

How to use tropospheric ducting effect

The effect of tropospheric ducting is that the signal can travel in which services can be received differently. Another use of the tropospheric ducting effect is that if a similar frequency occurs, it can lead to co-channel interference.

This normally causes a short-term loss of reception or two radio services to be listened to at the same time. The extra signals can as well cause problems with relay transmitters in some network systems.

Using Meteor Scatter

Meteor scatter communication is a form of radio propagation often used by HAM radio operators. Using meteor scatter, HAM radio operators can improve HAM radio and also other profitable radio communications contacts to be prepared over distances reaching the range of 2000 km on the VHF bands.

Meteor scatter is also among the ionosphere whereby meteor strikes have left an influence. This can result in radio and laser intrusion and it is popular in areas with a lot of proximity to the poles and the Equator.

CHAPTER ELEVEN

What leads to meteoric trails?

Meteoric trails are majorly utilized by meteor scatter radio signal propagation once the meteor finds its way into the Earth's atmosphere. When the atmosphere looks to be more solid, the meteors catch up as the abrasion rises. The meteors enter the atmosphere at a given speed range of about 10 to 80 kilometers per second and they usually burn up and form trail elevations starting from 85 to 120 kilometers, depending on factors such as speed, size, and angle of entry.

As a matter of fact, meteor trails can also be used for radio signal propagation. Meteor trails can easily be seen just by looking up to the sky in the night and it's mostly during the period of meteor showers. Meteor trails allow for relevant communications to be provided or established through the use of special characteristics of the propagation. Additionally, they can be broken down into two densities of electrons which are **"Under dense"** and **"over dense"**.

Using Amplitude Modulation

Amplitude modulation is known to be the original kind of transmission that carries sounds. In recent times, amplitude modulation is still used sometimes in HAM radio. It also transmits sound in different voice communication over the radio. Moreover, it is not anywhere closer to efficiency in terms of other types of modulation, it is also been heard sometimes in amateur radio bands today.

The thought behind amplitude modulation is very simple and easy, the audio or the rest of modulating signal is used to diverge the amplitude of the carrier or RF signal.

There is a disadvantage to amplitude modulation which is the rate of low efficiency.

(NB: Amplitude modulation is a form of modulation that makes use of fixed frequency carrier wave which now has the amplitude or intensity of the signal modulated following the wave-form of the modulating (audio) signal).

CHAPTER TWELVE

All about QPR Operations

QRP, an acronym for amateur radio operation, gives a lot of difficulty for operating and for constructing which can be especially rewarding and exciting. QRP operation has a big and increasing band of radio HAM. QRP comes from the Q codes which were for Morse, CW, and other radio transmissions.

A few radio amateurs who have been licensed allow them to make use of the complete legal power mostly prefer QRP operation because it gives them a great sense of contentment and guarantees lots of new world challenges in the aspect of amateur radio operating and also building the equipment.

Using continuous wave transmission

Continuous-wave is the electromagnetic wave of continuous amplitude that is measured to be of infinite duration. An ancient way of radio transmission can as well be referred to as continuous wave *(NB: This is usually because a sinusoidal carrier wave is turned on and off).* Continuous-wave (CW) is also known as **"undamped wave".**

Information can be moved in the various duration of the on and off time of the signal. In recent times, HAM radio transceivers use solid-state components and microprocessors to assist specific communication modes including continuous wave CW, sound, picture, and plenty of digital data modes. The continuous wave was introduced shortly after the damped wave became very broad, inefficient, and not reliable for communicating.

Finally, continuous wave (CW) Consists of vacuum tube oscillators that could be reliable based on the very pure note. The Laser output is usually permanent over seconds or higher and it is an example of continuous-wave transmission.

How to use Repeaters

Repeaters can receive frequency signals and also send signals using another frequency. The frequency which it receives is called the input frequency while on the other hand; the frequency it transmits to can be referred to as output frequency.

In other to use a repeater, a transceiver is needed; the transceiver will be able to transmit on the repeater's input frequency and can receive on the repeater's output frequency as well. Repeater frequency is mostly indicated in the form of the output frequency and the offset. Your transmitter controls the frequency that is dissimilar from the frequency that is received by the offset amount.

Whenever you start your first FM repeater contact in HAM radio, you are expected to practice most repeater operating technique and skills *(NB: Be aware that it won't take much of your time to hear and acquaint yourself with the steps used by most HAMS in your region, Although, accepted steps can be different a little from repeater to repeater).*

To also use amateur radio repeater, here are a few tips which should be followed, so you can actually get the right way in using amateur radio repeater

- **Pay attention:** Before using an amateur repeater as a beginner, it is always good to hear first. Repeaters are mostly different from the way they operate, so hearing allows you to know how the repeater is being operated and more about how the other stations in amateur radio make use of it.

- **CQ calls not permitted:** Firstly, confirm that the CQ calls are not produced through repeaters. Instead, stations broadcast that they are "listening through" the repeater.

Other tips include:

- **Check the CTCSS tone:** Make sure the CTCSS tone is correct.

- Give portable and mobile stations sufficient attention
- Don't talk for long periods
- Wait before transmitting in a contact

CHAPTER THIRTEEN

How to install a transceiver in a car

To install a radio transceiver in your car, there are numerous steps to follow. While some steps might be easy, others may be difficult. Here are the steps to follow to install transceivers in a car:

- **Know your car**

HAM radio transceivers have different types; however, everything can be classified as transceivers because they operate by sending and receiving on a similar range and frequency. Additionally, the transceiver's range and power ranking will confirm how to pick a HAM radio transceiver for your vehicle.

A vehicle that has programmed transmission and labor-intensive transmissions are similar. The two utilize one radio band and their level of power output is high when in use. A car with programmed transmission makes use of transceivers that transmits on 860 MHz, while the manual transmission transmits on 815 MHz.

The majority of HAMS practice all modes of operation, while you can find a few HAM radio transceivers which can only transmit and cannot receive. This mostly happens to street-legal cars. You will rarely find ham radios that can receive and as well transmit in Automatic mode. They mostly have a transceiver that can do just one which is transmitted.

- **Alter the radio unit's antenna**

Ham radio transceivers can also be classified as antennas. Your vehicle radio must have a replaceable antenna that is similar to a mobile phone antenna, which accepts the radio to receive radio waves and accept the radio to link to an antenna for transmission. If you don't have an antenna in a car radio, you can as well utilize a small or plexiglass antenna.

- **Proceed to install your transceiver**

Once you have brought out the radio unit's old antenna, ensure you cut the wire and place the new antenna in position. Users can utilize a little screwdriver to bring out the receiver's fuse. Once done, you can now put your transceiver to your vehicle's power supply.

After this process, you can now do the following steps:

- Install your transceiver's power cable

- Touch your car Bluetooth frequency

- Generate a PIN for your mobile phone

- Sync to Android Auto

- Use your mobile phone to navigate and it works as an assistant

- Benefit from hands-free phone

How to use a Slow-Scan TV

Slow-scan television (SSTV) is a method of video communication in which a succession of fixed pictures is sent and gotten at periods. SSTV is pragmatic for transmission of pictures over regular telephone utility (POTS) lines and in different apps where the accessible transfer speed is seriously restricted.

Slow-scan TV was utilized to send the primary video pictures back to earth from the Apollo 11 moon mission. Slow scan television is now and then utilized in security systems, medical imaging, and the remote observing of unsafe equipment. Novice radio operators rarely use SSTV in their communications. A majority of SSTV communication is completed in grayscale.

A Slow scan television signal comprises a fast arrangement of sound tones having variable pitch. When it is heard directly, it has a trademark chattering sound. An SSTV communication station comprises a phone communication or radio transceiver, a program known as a sweep converter, a camcorder, and a PC. As a result, a scan converter uses two data converters, one for getting through the mouthpiece or line input port and the other one for communicating through the speaker or line yield port.

The scan converter alters approaching SSTV tones into pictures appropriate for viewing on the PC. These pictures can be seen in real-time, kept away independently, or saved as an arrangement of video documents.

CHAPTER FOURTEEN

How to use Gridlock Operator

Here are the steps to go about this process:

- **Hit the search button:** After you have entered the search button, the map will move into the location that it found and place a pin at this location.

- **Find the closest town:** Look towards the top bar of the grid locator to find a search button that allows the map to show the nearest location it could see for the city, area, address, longitude, and latitude entered.

- **Move over to property:** To change the location or change to the property, simply use the direction buttons on the regulator located at the upper left of the map.

- **Enter a point on property:** To put a pin on a particular location clicking on the map is required. The grid ID and some information concerning that location will be viewed in the panel on the left-hand side. You can as well select multiple locations by pressing the icon at the upper left of the map. Also, you can click on another icon at the upper left of the map to choose Regions.

- **Print view for records:** Tap or touch the **"Print"** link situated at the top right-hand side of the map. At this point, it will automatically create a new print window.

- **Choose tools to view data:** Usually, you would find a link on the left panel, below the information for the chosen pin that allows you to create tools to show data for the recent location.

How to set up Transceivers

Step by step instructions to set up transceivers are made available below:

If you choose to set up a transceiver, there are countless things one should take care of or ensure everything is in wonderful condition to avoid potential risk. Likewise, ensure that there is an elastic security cap accessible to consistently manage the transceiver. In the wake of taking such security measures, you can push forward in setting up a transceiver.

There are numerous radio transceivers and you simply need to realize which is best for you. This section will discuss the Juniper Networks devices and how to set them up which are as per the following:

The transceivers for Juniper Networks devices are heated insertable field replaceable units and heated removable: you could continually bring it out without having to switch off the device or stop the flow of its functions.

- After inserting a transceiver or after you change the media type setup, you will at that point, be patient for a minimum of six seconds so the interface can display operational commands.

- It is prudent you utilize just optical connectors and optical transceivers purchased from Juniper Networks alongside your Juniper Network device.

CHAPTER FIFTEEN

HAM Radio Tips and Tricks for

Beginner Operators

Assembling your first HAM radio station can be energizing, confounding, and perplexing. However, do not worry because we will provide you with the basic HAM radio tips and tricks in which operators can use to build and use their HAM radio station. Additionally, the stated tips here might be of help to you because it is likely to save you time and cost, as well.

1. Be adaptable

The first tip and trick for HAM radio operators are to be adaptable and flexible. Also, try not to expect that you will be performing similar exercises on the air until the end of time.

Here are a couple of tips on adaptability:

- Try not to utilize specialized gear until you are pretty sure it is needed for a particular kind of operation or work.
- Utilize a PC and programming for things that are probably going to change, such as working on the computerized modes.
- Try not to disregard establishing and holding — assemble this in as the initial step. It is much difficult to do if you ignore it in the beginning and having it set up makes it simple to change the hardware format.
- Attempt an alternate layout to check whether something works much better. Just so you know, you are permitted to adjust your perspective. You may discover another course of action to be more agreeable or helpful.

- Leave some spending plan for shocks, like a power distribution or special cable.

2. Study different stations

Scrutinize and examine the internet for write-ups and recordings that show how different stations are assembled and run. Also, endeavor to write a note of brilliant ideas. Try not to be scared by large stations, since they all began as little stations.

Furthermore, try not to stop for a second to contact the station operators with questions; this is because they will answer any reasonable question you may have. Make the most of your youthful days to visit neighborhood stations, as well.

3. Find out about those additional capacities

Since you spent your hard-earned money for every one of those controls, you should figure out how they work and set them to work for you.

Here are some popular instances:

- **MON:** An acronym for Monitor, this option is typically near a handheld transceiver's PTT switch. Here's what it does: It opens the squelch so you can tune in for a feeble station without altering the standard squelch level.

- **Memory writes:** You should work on moving your VFO settings to a memory channel. On VHF/UH, this is acceptable practice for public help operation. On HF, you can utilize this while pursuing a DXpedition or making a timetable. Try to figure out how to do this without alluding to the manual.

- **Noise reduction and noise blankers:** Activating and deactivating this function is simple, however, did you realize they are customizable? Controlling the sensitivity of these capacities modifies them for the noise in your area. You ought to likewise be gifted at changing the radio's RF gain and AGC for HF activity. Ensure you are aware of where the preamp and attenuator controls are, as well.

- **Flexible filters:** Since a majority of new radios utilize DSP, filters are easily customizable, can be balanced above and underneath your operating frequency, and various settings put away for some time in the future. After you learn how to use these functions, you can't help thinking about how you lived without them for a long time.

- **Voice and Morse messages:** A lot of radios can keep/save messages and play them back. In a case whereby you are working in a challenge, this capacity is exceptionally convenient. A few radios can record sound behind closed doors, as well. While you're grinding away, figure out how to utilize your radio's inner Morse keyer.

- **Custom arrangements:** Your radio might have the option to save its operating configuration on a memory card or inside. This permits you to make custom arrangements for easygoing operation, public assistance nets, challenging, portable operation, etc.

4. Shop for utilized equipment

If you have a learned companion who can assist you with evading exhausted and insufficient gear, purchasing used equipment is an extraordinary method to begin HAM radio stations. Buying used gear from a seller who offers a guarantee is additionally a decent alternative.

Setting aside cash currently leaves you more money for investigating new modes and groups later.

- **Caveat emptor:** You can without much stress experience out-of-date or ineffectively working equipment when you're looking for used equipment. In case you are in doubt or if you can't look at it, or if the arrangement appears to be unrealistic, leave it behind.

5. Assemble something yourself

Utilizing equipment that you construct yourself is a blast. Start little by building accessory projects, for example, sound switches, keyers, and filters. Building things without any help can help you save a little bit of cash. Try not to be reluctant to get out the drill and binding iron. Finally, you can discover several web articles, magazines, and books of different projects to kick you off.

6. Optimize your signal

Ensure you are utilizing your keyer, microphone, and sound card appropriately. Get along with a companion and arrange your sound so that it's reasonable, clean, and seems like you.

Note down how the ALC and force yield meters act when you have things set appropriately. For FM voice, discover what mouthpiece direction and voice level sound best. Have your companion tune in to neighboring channels and frequencies — splattering or over-deviation squander control and bother others.

On the digital modes, check your sound settings, both transmit and receive. In terms of the receiver, your sound level ought to be well over the least noise level yet not so high that a solid sign surpasses the highest input range of the decoder. On the other hand, in terms of the transmit, have that accommodating companion be certain you don't overdrive the sound circuits and make fake signs.

Additionally, when utilizing an SSB handset for digital modes like PSK, RTTY, or one of the WSJT family, the ALC framework, including speech processing, ought to be turned off. Meanwhile, if you can't turn ALC totally off, set your sound level so the ALC meter shows no action during transmissions. ALC changes the sign level, contorting the tweak and making it harder to decipher.

7. Set aside money by building your cables

You require heaps of cables and connectors in your station. At an expense of generally $5 or more for each premade cable, you can rapidly spend as much on connecting your gear as possible on buying significant equipment. Figure out how to install your own connectors on cables, and you will save a lot of money throughout your ham profession. Additionally, you'll be better ready to investigate and carry out repairs as at when due.

8. Construct bit by bit

After you have the essentials of your station set up, redesign your equipment in advance so you can generally hear somewhat farther than you can send. Plan with an objective so your HAM radio money and time dedicated to all work does not go in vain.

9. Track down the most fragile connection

Each station has a frail connection. Continuously be watching out for a plausible place of disappointment or of quality loss. On the wireless transmissions, you will experience stations with a multipacks radio yet a modest, carport deal receiver that outcomes in muted or contorted sound. Utilize quality stuff, and keep intensely utilized equipment very much kept up.

10.   Comfort yourself

You will spend a ton of hours before your radio, so you need to be comfortable, as well. Start with a comfortable seat. Nice seats are regularly accessible in used office-furniture stores at good discounts. Likewise, ensure that you have sufficient lighting and that the working work area is a bit high.

What are DX clusters?

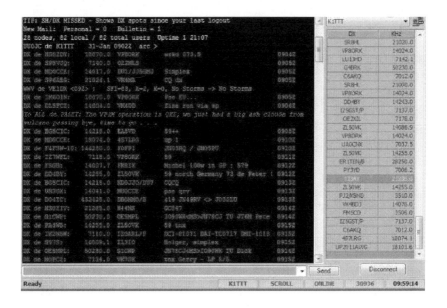

In a nutshell, DX Clusters is a node into which new DX hunters can post details related to DX. Meanwhile, in physical terms, a DX cluster is a central PC that accumulates/ gathers, keeps, and gives out information that HAMS delivers to it.

You can find thousands of nodes worldwide, which are connected through the radio or internet. Basically, connections made to clusters are usually done through packet radio or telnet.

The scenario in which several networks of DX clusters are connected is the most powerful characteristic because it provides newbies nearly immediate access to information about uncommon and scarce DX conditions like VHF ducting and meteor scatter.

More so, people who use clusters will utilize PC software that can communicate with the cluster. On the first login, users will be prompted to give our station information *(NB: As a result, it permits other HAMs to compare DX openings to their physical stand, thereby making informed declarations concerning beam direction).*

How to set up SDR Transceivers

SDR is an acronym for Software Defined Radio. In SDR, RF communications are carried out with firmware and software, to deliver signals information which is always processed by the hardware. Furthermore, this hardware is a combination of amplifiers, demodulators, mixers, filters, modulators, and so much more.

Hence, SDR only utilizes a DAC and ADC to carry out Analog to Digital and Digital to Analog signal change alongside antennas, without having to use a lot of hardware devices. As a result, it makes SDR very flexible and easy to correct.

SDR is divided into:

- SDR Receivers: This can only receive radio signals.
- SDR Transceivers: This kind can both send and receive radio signals.

Pros and Cons of SDR

Pros

- Can get a high-performance level
- Can alter performance level by updating the software
- Can utilize similar hardware for a lot of different radios
- Can reconfigure radios by simply updating software

Cons

- Software and hardware abilities are needed to develop an SDR
- The basic platform might be costly for easy radios

CHAPTER SIXTEEN

Equipment needed to set up an SDR

After learning what SFR is all about, here's what you need to set up an SDR:

1. SDR
2. Antennas: If you decide to use an SDR transceiver or receiver, you must ensure you connect antennas to transmit and receive radio signals for a long time.
3. Computer Running SDR software: Multiple types of SDR software can be used on your radio. Some of which are outlined below:
   - Linrad
   - Studio1
   - SDR
   - HDSDR
   - GQRX
   - SDRUno

Things you can do with the SDR

Here are a couple of things users can explore and do with the SDR:

1. Amateur radio
2. Know how Global Navigation Satellite Systems is operated
3. Build a GSM network
4. Receive broadcast radio
5. Follow aircraft through mode S transmissions
6. Follow ships through AIS transmissions
7. Radio astronomy
8. Test with LTE
9. Set up a DRM transmitter.

Setting up your personal SDR doesn't require you to spend too much because tuners are dependent on the Realtek RTL282U chip and can only allow radio signals; which do not transmit.

Private activities for HAM operators

HAM operators are people who make use of tools in a HAM radio to join in a double-sided way private communications with other HAM operators on radio frequencies given to the HAM radio service. Although Ham operators do have some private activities where only HAMS can understand or be involved in, and that is the more reason why HAM radio operators must obtain a license from the executive governing authority.

As a part of their license, HAM radio operators are given a call sign, and it allows them to know one another during the process of communication. A statistics was done over the year and brought out a database which says that there are over 3 million HAM radio operators all over the world.

According to reports, it was gathered that not all government maintains full demographic statistics of their amateur radio operator population. From findings and research, the main part of countries in the world in which Amateur radio operators are from is mostly the USA, North America, Europe, and East Asia.

Meanwhile, in Yemen and North Korea, their government has banned their citizens not to be amateur radio operators. Also, as a ham radio operator, there are a few countries whereby obtaining an amateur radio license is very difficult because of the bureaucratic system or it's very expensive to purchase or acquire.

CONCLUSION

As we conclude this guide, HAM radio is the perfect choice of communication for your household and your workplace. The radio allows you to communicate with your family and friends from far and wide.

This book was written to educate you on everything there is to know about HAM radio, its uses, and how it can benefit people all around the world. At the end of this guide, you should be equipped with the right information that will make you a pro in using HAM radio. The information contained in this guide is filled with a proper explanation, a step-by-step guide, and a proper illustration that ensures you have gotten value for your money.

ABOUT THE AUTHOR

Curtis Campbell is an intelligent and innovative computer scientist with experience in software engineering. As a renowned technology expert, his passion for capturing still photos and motion pictures has led him into photography and videography, which he is doing with excellence. Curtis has produced several tutorials on different topics. As a researcher and a prolific writer with proficiency in handling tech products, he learned different approaches to managing issues on the internet and other applications.

Curtis Campbell

Made in United States
Troutdale, OR
11/12/2024

24705222R00062